JESUS RETURNS TO HEAVEN

Matthew 28:11–20
Luke 24:36–53
Acts 1:1–12 for Children

Written by Robert Baden
Illustrated by Michael Hackett

ARCH ® Books
Copyright © 1995 Concordia Publishing House
3558 S. Jefferson Avenue, St. Louis, MO 63118-3968
Manufactured in the United States of America

Jesus rose on Easter Day
Alive, no longer dead;
Though many heard the news with joy,
Some doubted what was said.

"Did Jesus really die?" they asked;
"Did Jesus really rise?"
And those who wanted Jesus dead
Created evil lies.

"No, Jesus didn't really rise,"
These evil people said;
"His body was removed at night,
But Jesus is still dead."

So everyone would know the truth,
Our Lord took forty days
To show He was indeed alive
In many different ways:

He walked, He talked, He ate, He showed
His wounded hands and side;
And soon the truth of Easter Day
Had traveled far and wide.

Then Jesus said, "All power on earth
And heaven belongs to Me;
Soon I'll send special power to you
So all of you can be

"My messengers throughout the world;
Here's what I hope you'll do:
Go share with everyone the love
That I have shared with you.

"First tell those in Jerusalem,
Then all in every land,
That I have lived and died for them;
Make sure they understand.

"Make them disciples, teach them how
To live; and when that's done
Baptize them in the name of God—
Father, Spirit, Son."

Then Jesus smiled and said, "My friends,
This promise now I give:
I'll be with you each hour and day
As long as you will live.

"Wait until the Spirit comes
To give My power to you;
Once He has come—it won't be long—
You'll know just what to do."

Then Jesus led His faithful friends
To a hill outside of town.
And there He smiled and hugged each one
And asked them to sit down.

He blessed them all, raised up His hands,
And before their very eyes,
Began to lift up off the ground
And rise into the skies!

His friends jumped quickly to their feet
And shouted loud and long!
They kept on watching till their Lord
Was hidden by a cloud.

"I can't believe it!" one man said,
Gazing toward the sky.
"What does this mean?" another cried,
"Why did He leave us? Why?"

All kept on looking at the spot
Where Jesus disappeared,
When suddenly they sensed that someone
Else had just appeared.

There standing by them were two men,
Both dressed in shining white;
"Why are you looking up?" one asked;
"Everything's all right.

"Yes, Jesus now has left the earth,
But He'll come again one day;
And then He'll take all who believe
To heaven with Him to stay."

This message filled their hearts with joy;
How glad they were to hear it!
They worshiped God and went to wait
For the coming Holy Spirit.

Dear Parents:

Help your child find Ascension Day—40 days after Easter—on a calendar. Circle the date and plan a special celebration for that day. As you plan, discuss the Great Commission—Jesus' command to His disciples and to us to proclaim His Gospel in our own community and throughout the world.

Roleplay witnessing your faith with your child. Then decide on someone in your neighborhood with whom you can share God's love. Give that person a homemade gift or card, expressing Jesus' care and sharing your faith in Him.

If your church uses offering envelopes, show one to your child. Explain that part of the money you give in the offering helps missionaries proclaim the good news that Jesus died and rose again for all people. Decide on a way your child can earn money to support world mission work.

Pray with your child and thank Jesus for getting your rooms ready in heaven. Ask the blessing of His Holy Spirit as you share your faith with your child, your neighbors, and people throughout the world.

The Editor